BARRACUDA VS. MORAY EEL

BY KIERAN DOWNS

BELLWETHER MEDIA • MINNEAPOLIS, MN

T0014865

Torque brims with excitement
perfect for thrill-seekers of all kinds.
Discover daring survival skills, explore
uncharted worlds, and marvel at mighty
engines and extreme sports. In *Torque* books,
anything can happen. Are you ready?

This edition first published in 2022 by Bellwether Media, Inc.

No part of this publication may be reproduced in whole or in part without written
permission of the publisher. For information regarding permission, write to
Bellwether Media, Inc., Attention: Permissions Department,
6012 Blue Circle Drive, Minnetonka, MN 55343.

Library of Congress Cataloging-in-Publication Data

 LC record for Barracuda vs. Moray Eel available
at https://lccn.loc.gov/2021039743

Editor: Rebecca Sabelko   Designer: Josh Brink

Printed in the United States of America, North Mankato, MN.

TABLE OF CONTENTS

THE COMPETITORS

The **coral reef** is home to dangerous **predators**. Barracudas are one of them. They are among the reef's strongest swimmers. These speedy fish can chase down almost any **prey**.

But barracudas have challengers. Moray eels use sneak attacks. They snatch up prey that swim by. Which fish would win in a reef battle?

Barracudas live in warm oceans around the world. They hunt in shallow waters and coral reefs. They feast upon fish of all sizes.

Barracudas have pointed heads and long, slim bodies. They are covered in silver scales. Large barracudas can be almost 10 feet (3 meters) long. Some weigh up to 110 pounds (50 kilograms).

GREAT BARRACUDA

SOMETHING SHINY

Barracudas use their sense of sight to hunt. They chase after shiny fish. Barracudas may also attack shiny objects worn by divers!

GREAT BARRACUDA PROFILE

0 FEET	2 FEET	4 FEET	6 FEET	8 FEET	10 FEET

LENGTH
ALMOST 10 FEET
(3 METERS)

WEIGHT
UP TO 110 POUNDS
(50 KILOGRAMS)

HABITAT

CORAL REEFS

OPEN OCEANS

GREAT BARRACUDA RANGE

☐ RANGE

GIANT MORAY EEL PROFILE

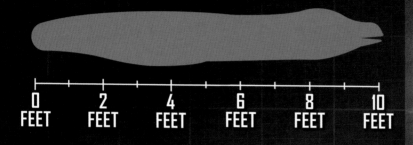

```
0       2       4       6       8       10
FEET    FEET    FEET    FEET    FEET    FEET
```

LENGTH
ALMOST 10 FEET
(3 METERS)

WEIGHT
AROUND 66 POUNDS
(30 KILOGRAMS)

HABITAT

CORAL REEFS

GIANT MORAY EEL RANGE

☐ RANGE

Moray eels are mostly found in warm oceans. They live in small **crevices** along shorelines and coral reefs. Morays are the only fish that can swim backward!

Moray eels have snakelike bodies coated in **mucus**. A long **dorsal fin** runs along their back. There are hundreds of moray eel **species**. Some are colorful. They may have patterns, too.

DORSAL FIN

GIANT MORAY EEL

GET CLEAN

Moray eels often visit cleaning stations. Small fish and shrimp eat tiny, harmful animals off eels' skin.

SECRET WEAPONS

Many moray eels are **nocturnal** hunters. They have **adapted** a strong sense of smell. This allows the eels to find prey in the dark.

BARRACUDA SWIM SPEED

20
10 30
0 40

20
10 30
0 40

**36 MILES
(58 KILOMETERS)
PER HOUR**

**6 MILES
(9.7 KILOMETERS)
PER HOUR**

BARRACUDA

HUMAN

Barracudas use speed to be successful
hunters. They can swim up to 36 miles
(58 kilometers) per hour. When barracudas
see shiny fish, they easily chase after them.

Barracudas have two rows of teeth. Small outer teeth cut prey. Long inner teeth stick into prey. Fish cannot escape!

1 INCH

0.5 INCHES

0

0.8"

FANGTOOTH MORAY EEL TOOTH

UP TO 0.8 INCHES
(2 CENTIMETERS)

Moray eels have two sets of jaws. Sharp, backward-pointing teeth in the outer jaw hold prey. The inner jaw shoots from the throat. Then, it pulls food into the throat.

SECRET WEAPONS

SWIM SPEED

SHARP TEETH

SILVER SCALES

Barracudas often hunt in clear water near the surface of oceans. Their silver scales blend into the color of the water. This makes it hard for prey to spot them.

MORAY EEL

SENSE OF SMELL

TWO SETS
OF JAWS

CAMOUFLAGE

Moray eels are brightly colored. They blend into colorful coral reefs. This **camouflage** helps them hide from prey and predators.

ATTACK MOVES

Barracudas **ambush** their prey. Once fish get close, barracudas attack them with a burst of speed. Few fish can outswim barracudas!

Moray eels also use surprise attacks against prey. They hide in reefs and wait. When prey is near, morays spring from their hiding spots at high speeds.

CHANGING COLORS

Some moray eels can change color to blend in with coral reefs!

Barracudas attack with their mouths. Their strong jaws and sharp teeth hold onto prey. The teeth slice into their catch to wound it. They swallow smaller prey whole.

Some morays wrap their bodies around prey. Food cannot move or escape. Morays take small bites out of large prey. They swallow small animals whole.

READY, FIGHT!

A barracuda is on the hunt. It swims past a crevice in a coral reef. Suddenly, a moray eel strikes with its jaws wide open!

But the barracuda is too fast. With the eel in the open, the barracuda attacks. It sinks its teeth into the eel. The barracuda found its meal!

GLOSSARY

adapted—changed over a long period of time

ambush—to carry out a surprise attack

camouflage—coloring or markings that make animals look like their surroundings

coral reef—a structure made of coral that usually grows in shallow seawater

crevices—narrow openings in rocks or walls

dorsal fin—a flat, thin fin on the backs of some fish

mucus—a slimy substance that wets and protects skin

nocturnal—active at night

predators—animals that hunt other animals for food

prey—animals that are hunted by other animals for food

species—kinds of animals

TO LEARN MORE

AT THE LIBRARY

Adamson, Thomas K. *Great White Shark vs. Killer Whale.* Minneapolis, Minn.: Bellwether Media, 2020.

Buckley, James, Jr. *Dangerous Teeth!: Moray Eel Attack.* Minneapolis, Minn.: Bearport Publishing, 2021.

Hulick, Kathryn. *Coral Reefs.* New York, N.Y.: AV2, 2019.

ON THE WEB

FACTSURFER

Factsurfer.com gives you a safe, fun way to find more information.

1. Go to www.factsurfer.com

2. Enter "barracuda vs. moray eel" into the search box and click 🔍.

3. Select your book cover to see a list of related content.

INDEX

The images in this book are reproduced through the courtesy of: Fabien Monteil, front cover (barracuda); Joe Belanger, front cover (moray eel), 14 (silver scales); Istvan Kovacs, pp. 2-3, 20-24 (barracuda); WaterFrame_eda/ Alamy, pp. 2-3, 20-24 (moray eel); Malbert, p. 4; Alexandra HB, p. 5; Pally/ Alamy, pp. 6-7; Richard Whitcombe, pp. 8-9; Ellen Hui, p. 10; Peter Douglas Clark, p. 11; Dave Fleetham/ Pacific Stock/ SuperStock, p. 12; Natursports, p. 13; J.W.Alker/ Westend61/ SuperStock, p. 14; Kristina Vackova, p. 14 (swim speed); Joost van Uffelen, p. 14 (sharp teeth); Izen Kai, p. 15; yeshaya dinerstein, p. 15 (sense of smell); Foodies Academy, p. 15 (two jaws); Elliotte Rusty Harold, p. 15 (camouflage); NHPA/Photoshot/ agefotostock, p. 16; SeaTops/imageBROKER/ SuperStock, p. 17; RainervonBrandis, p. 18; Norbert Probst/ Alamy, p. 19.